Driven
to Distraction

BY DANNY STURROCK AND MARK WHEELLER

dbda

Driven to Distraction by Danny Sturrock and Mark Wheeller

Commissioned by "Is this Fun For Everyone?"/Havering 16+ Transport Partnership

Acknowledgements:

Mike Lane (Is This Fun For Everyone?) who made this idea come to fruition.

"Is This Fun For Everyone?" & Havering 16+ Transport Partnership for both commissioning the play and funding the StopWatch Theatre Company tour.

Adrian New Producer StopWatch Theatre Company not only for making the first tour so successful but for enormous input to the early drafts of the script.

Marshalls Park School for their feedback on the first draft... and the unknown student who suggested Tab's name.

Dawn and Lynda from dbda who are always so willing to consider our plays for publication.

Sophie Gorrell Burnes and all at MBA for their continued support and belief.

Sources:

John and Dennis (East London Buses)

Bus Driver John Norris (Nobby) who has acted as consultant throughout the script development

Dave from Epping (Quenchers research!)

Joe & Katy from Southampton

ISBN 978 1 902843 28 5

BRITISH LIBRARY CATALOGUING IN PUBLICATION DATA
A catalogue record for this book is available from the British Library.

Sophie Gorell Barnes, MBA Literary Agents Limited, 62 Grafton Way, London. W1P 5LD.
Tel: 020 7387 2076. Email Sophie@mbalit.co.uk

Further copies of this publication can be purchased from:
dbda, Pin Point, Rosslyn Crescent, Harrow HA1 2SU.
Tel: 0870 333 7771   Fax: 0870 333 7772   E-mail: info@dbda.co.uk

Introduction

As soon as the suggestion of writing a play about anti-social behaviour on buses was made I knew it was an opportunity for Danny and I to work together on our first script collaboration. I phoned him and he seemed up for it... (it's always easy to convince someone when it's a commission because money is involved!). I knew any play we produced would benefit from his talent with multi-media... but that is far from all that Danny contributed to this project.

Once we had outlined the idea of the script and the innovative structure (based on an idea from a script I'd read on a writing course I was doing at the Nuffield Theatre in Southampton at the time) we made a decision to have only four characters appear in the play. We each took control of two of them. Danny being the youngest (by 20 years!), voiced the two teenagers in the play. I have always been impressed by Danny's ability to give words to teenagers that don't sound like "teacher impersonating young people". Meanwhile I took on writing the roles of Zinc and Jo, who I imagined to be approximately my age (50 at that time). We wrote all the scenes separately with the exception of the final crash scene on which we collaborated at the end of the writing process. We checked each others work and made suggestions about how to improve, but in essence the voices of the older remained mine and the younger Danny's.

I soon discovered that this had the disadvantage of knowing whose work was being criticised when comments came back. It seemed always to be the writing of Zinc and Jo, particularly in the lead up to the professional performances (StopWatch Theatre Company) that came in for the worst criticisms. I re-wrote those scenes many, many times, while Danny's scenes seemed to me to be pretty much right from the start.

Zinc in particular came in for some strong criticism as he was "moaning all the time". It was a difficult criticism to address as the situation he was in would lead most to moan! It made Danny and I question whether or not we were happy with the structure... if we changed that we could easily show Zinc prior to the accident when he could be far more positive. We decided to keep the structure as we felt it would drive towards the accident. I am glad to say I think we were right. I also know that Adrian New's (StopWatch producer) comments helped me to focus on making Zinc more "interesting" and positive.

Introduction

There was about a three month gap from finishing writing D2D, as we called it, to seeing it in performance... enough time for me to forget the details. When we saw it performed by StopWatch I remember being pleasantly surprised... it worked! Some parts we had stood by (e.g. the whole sub plot re Zinc's history) worked particularly well in our opinion. This back story had been criticised throughout as being perhaps too controversial. Danny and I stood firm and it certainly benefits the uncomfortable feeling leading to the climatic crash scene.

The other aspect which I know caused difficulties for StopWatch was the inclusion of multi-media. This became a strong feature of their production and almost made it seem 3D! I would advise any prospective director to get hold of the Multimedia disk Danny has made and find a way of incorporating it into any production you do... it will be worthwhile!

The other problem Adrian had with my scenes, even after the performance, was that Jo was still little more than a foil for Zinc i.e. she didn't have a "life". I remember being deflated that yet again I hadn't quite cracked it... but once I sat at my computer with this criticism in mind many of the re-writes that had ended up in my "bin" came back to me. Things I knew had happened to Jo but that didn't get a mention in the script. Finally her character began to take off and I am now really pleased with this final version for dbda.

Danny and I were keen to produce something that was different from our other output and I wanted to do a play where we had few characters and the story is told through predominantly naturalistic dialogue. This was a challenge (particularly for me) and one I found very difficult at times. It transpires to be a very "different" play with new challenges for anyone who chooses to present it. We know it works because we had the honour of seeing an excellent professional version of an earlier draft... so it has been road tested.

We are also pleased to suggest a shorter version (below) which can be presented for examination purposes.

Good luck to anyone who puts it on.

With GCSE in mind a solid and understandable version of this play can be performed within the time constraints by only performing Sections 3, 4, 5 & 11. This should run (2m/2f) for about 20 minutes.

Mark Wheeller

Introduction

Having been a student of Mark's some 11 years ago and having followed the success of his writing since then I was really pleased when he approached me with the idea of writing this piece together. However, it then very quickly dawned on me that I would be writing with someone who has had massive success and really knows what they are doing... I couldn't help considering myself to be somewhat of an amateur in comparison to Mark! However, I gladly took up Mark's offer and was looking forward to seeing how someone with experience goes about writing a play from scratch.

Not only was this a 'first' for me in terms of writing with Mark, but having always written about an idea I had conceived myself it was somewhat alien to me to be writing for someone else. From the outset, with everything I had written up to this point, I had always had it in my mind to produce and direct the plays myself, but this was going to be someone else's job.

There was another problem; the subject of the piece was to be about anti-social behaviour on buses. Having already written a play (Bang Out of Order) with Johnny Carrington about anti-social behaviour, I was keen that this should not become a carbon copy, but be completely fresh... I needn't have worried, they are totally different!

I was also keen to be able to inject the use of music and multi-media into the piece, as I have done with my other works in recent years. Not only did I want the multi-media to serve as a digital set, but I wanted to find a way in which the characters on stage could interact with it. I had an idea of graffiti being sprayed which would appear on screen as the actor stood in front of it miming, which would make it seem as if they were actually spraying the words. Once this idea had come to mind, the others soon followed.

Mark and I got together and talked about how we could structure the piece. Mark mentioned a technique where a story is told from two sides, starting in different timeframes, which at some point meet. I instantly liked the sound of this and we decided to go with it and see what happened.

Part of the original plan for this piece was that, once written, it could be produced for a tour into schools within Havering. So with this in mind Mark and I decided that the cast would need to be small, with no more than 4 actors required, as this would better suit a touring company. We then settled on having only 4 physical characters,

Introduction

although there is a fifth character that is given a voice through the other 4 characters but never seen.

We began by interviewing London bus drivers and a group of young people, some of whom had firsthand experience of anti-social behaviour on buses. Once the interviews had been typed up we set about writing the first scenes. It had all gone so well so far, would this be the point at which it went wrong? Would Mark hate what I was writing, would our styles of writing completely clash? To my relief, it was easy! We both liked what the other was doing and the two differing styles gelled together brilliantly. We worked independently of each other on each scene, apart from the final one which we both wrote together, and before we knew it, we had a first complete draft.

Once the play script had been submitted I set about working on the multi-media elements and original soundtrack. By this point Stopwatch Theatre Company had been employed to tour the play in schools within Havering and were able to provide valuable input into how they would like the multi-media elements to work for them in the context of a performance.

The process of getting D2D (as it became known to us) to the format it is today has been very much a team effort, and having seen the piece bought to life on stage I'm really pleased with the end result.

I hope that any groups who go on to use this piece in the future enjoy working with it as much as I have.

Danny Sturrock

First performed by StopWatch Theatre Company in May 2009.

Cast: (In order of appearance)

Tabs	**Anthony Rotsa**
Emma	**Liz Hollis**
Zinc	**Peter McCamley and David John Watton**
Jo	**Lynsey Garvey**
Directed by	**Julie Addy**
Produced by	**Adrian New**

Cast List

Cast list : (In order of appearance)

Tabs

Emma   Tabs' girlfriend

Zinc   Bus driver

Jo   Zinc's wife

Media 1: *A clock showing 6:45 is displayed as the play begins and then the image zooms out to reveal the wall of Jo and Zinc's Living room.*

Jo:	*(On a mobile)* Hi love, what's up? I've had three missed calls from you.
Zinc:	*(On a mobile)* Jo, I'll be a bit late home.
Jo:	You OK?
Zinc:	I'm at the hospital… had a bit of a bump… in the bus… they want to check me over but don't fret, I'm fine.
Jo:	Do you want me to come?
Zinc:	No, 's fine.
Jo:	You can get home OK?
Zinc:	Yeh… ooh… I'm just being called… better go…
Jo:	See you in a while then?
Zinc:	Yeh… got to switch my phone off… see you.
Jo:	Sure you're OK.
Zinc:	I'm fine.
Jo:	Zed… *(Reaslises he's put the phone down. Somewhat sadly.)*… I had something to tell you too…

Music 1 /Media 2: The media in this section is made up of fast moving images, i.e. bus doors opening and closing, the 'stop' bell being pressed, London landmarks, High Street Shop signs, etc. the media fades to black as they board Zinc's bus.

A choreographed movement sequence showing Tabs and Emma travelling around the town on a bus, getting off at various stops to go shopping, get food, etc. They should appear very close and be having a lot of fun. The final time the couple board the bus they encounter Zinc, who is driving. The two parties recognise each other.

Zinc: You two been doing a bit of shopping have ya?

Emma: Just a bit.

Tabs: Well she has, I was just dragged around.

Emma: Liar! I'm not the one who spent an hour looking at hair gel! You big girl.

Zinc: Still keeping up your footy?

Tabs: Eh?

Zinc: Your football! Don't tell me you've stopped playing, you were blinding down the right wing if I remember right... it's the hair isn't it, that's why you don't recognise me...

Tabs: Hang on...

Zinc: Just try and imagine me a little slimmer... OK a lot slimmer, with the worst mullet you've ever seen!

Tabs: Yeh, I get ya... Zed innit?

Zinc: Well...well yeh, that's it.

Tabs: Zed used to coach the footy team I played for.

Emma: You played football?

Zinc: He was one of the best back then!

Tabs: Yeh but that was years ago... so why'd you cut the hair off? Midlife crisis?

Zinc: Something like that. It's good to see you, *(to Emma)* nice to meet you too love.

Emma:	And you.
Zinc:	Don't forget to swipe your Oysters.
Tabs:	Cheers Zed.
Zinc:	No worries.

There is the sound effect of the bus moving off. Tabs and Emma take a seat.

Media 3: *A still image of the interior of a bus to create a backdrop.*

Emma:	My feet are killing me!
Tabs:	I'm not surprised, we must have walked 12 miles!
Emma:	Don't exaggerate!

Tabs glances down and see something sticking out of Emma's bag.

Tabs:	What's that?
Emma:	What?
Tabs:	That drawing, in your bag.
Emma:	Oh… nothing, just a lil sketch.
Tabs:	Let's havva look then.
Emma:	No, it's crap trust me.
Tabs:	Oh, OK then.

The pair sit in silence for a moment before Tabs dives into her handbag and grabs her sketch. It's a design for a graffiti tag Emma has created.

Emma:	Oi you!
Tabs:	Well, well, well.
Emma:	See, told you it was crap!
Tabs:	Actually I'm impressed.
Emma:	Really.
Tabs:	Yeah… not a bad Tag… for a girl!

Emma:	*(Snatching it back from him.)* Cheeky git!
Tabs:	Only joking Babe.
Emma:	Better be. I've had a really nice day, thanks.
Tabs:	What you thanking me for?
Emma:	Would have been boring if you hadn't come with me.
Tabs:	Well that's OK. *(Sarcastically)* I've really enjoyed looking at shoes for 5 hours. I never knew there were so many different styles!
Emma:	Don't take the Mick! You loved it.
Tabs:	Yeh, but don't tell anyone, don't wanna ruin my rep!
Emma:	Heaven forbid... I can see it on the front of the Recorder tomorrow, "Local Bad Boy has shoe fetish"! Come on, you ain't that bad.
Tabs:	Not what everyone else thinks.
Emma:	You know all that stuff they were on about at school... kids doing stuff to the buses round our way and... everyone was saying you was one of em...
Tabs:	What if I was?
Emma:	They were saying you kept on pressing the emergency door stop buttons as they went past.
Tabs:	Yeh, funny eh? Really winds the drivers up that does, 'n' they never caught me. I'm just too good!
Emma:	I ain't got the bottle to do that stuff!
Tabs:	Little miss goody goody are ya?
Emma:	No! Not always.
Tabs:	Yeah right! You never get in trouble.
Emma:	I have been.
Tabs:	When?
Emma:	In year 8! I had an argument in Art with Alice Morgan and smashed up her papier mache fish!

Tabs: And?

Emma: And what?

Tabs: You mean that's it? You smashed up a paper fish!

Emma: I got a weeks detention for that!

Tabs: Ooooh check out Emma, master criminal!

Tabs begins tickling Emma.

Emma: *(Laughing)* Just stop.

There is a brief moment where the couples eyes meet. They slowly lean in for a kiss but just as their lips are about to meet the bus screeches to a halt and the pair are thrown forward in their seats.

Zinc: *(Shouting)* What do you think you're doing?
              (To the passengers) Sorry about that, is everyone OK?

Tabs: Cor, that was a bit close!

Media 4: *Backdrop of Zinc's Living room. There is a holiday brochure placed prominently in the room.*

Jo: Is that you Zed?

Zinc: *(Entering)* Yeh.

Jo: You alright?

Zinc: I can't believe a day could get this bad!
               (Seeing he needs support Jo goes to hug him)
               I might have killed someone.

Jo: Babe... I thought you said you'd just had a bump.
               I would have...

Zinc: I didn't want you to fret.

Jo: Sit down love.

Music 2 / Media 4: *Choppy/Distorted CCTV Style images are shown on screen, mixed with exterior images of a bus in motion. The pace of the images will build with the tension in the following monologue The images will then settle back to the backdrop of Zinc's lounge.*

Zinc: No. It's... *(Zinc tells the story gathering pace as it goes on. Music underscores this speech with CCTV style images playing in the background. Echo's of 'young' laughter and Zinc shouting at them to stop etc. as he recalls the situation in his head.)...* Look... there were these two kids in the back of the bus... they were... you know messing around. I knew one from football... Tabs... used to play for us when he was a Junior. I don't know what was up today... he was a good lad, and since I've been on this route I've seen him a few times, but today he was being a bloody idiot! He had a water pistol and was shooting it about and I thought he was gonna start on some kids who were there from the Special school... so
               I just shouted "Pack it in!". The cheeky sod turns round and says "Or what?". Then he swore at me! Couldn't believe it... I mean I know him... but he was walking up towards the cab and... can't remember exactly what he said... but, he was threatening. I only looked up at the screen for a few seconds and the car in front must have pulled up sharp and...

Jo:	You hit it.
Zinc:	Yeh. It spun off the road and smashed into some scaffolding on the front of the shops and it just gave way like matchsticks...
Jo:	Oh my word Zed... was anyone hurt?
Zinc:	A teenager in the car… it'll be in the papers tomorrow 'cos she's an MC. She was on her way to some press conference… she's got a new tune out. It didn't look good Jo. You know what's really bad? No one else bloody did anything about the lad on the bus... everyone else was…
Jo:	Turning a blind eye?
Zinc:	Yeh. They just expected me to sort him!
	(Pause)
Jo:	Every day you come home with horror stories… being abused… spat at… eggs… stones hurled at the bus… I mean golf clubs one time you said!
Zinc:	I know, but I knew this kid and he knew me! He's alright normally!
Jo:	Nothing ever happens! They always say they're just "messing around" and "messing around" makes it sound so innocent.
	(Pause)
	So, what happens now then… you know… with you… what 'bout work?
Zinc:	Still got to go in… won't be driving… cleaning, or painting white lines in the garage, things like that… I've got to make the best of it Jo… I mean, I can't just turn back time… change the date… not even change it… just go back to breakfast time… breakfast time would be OK… lunch even… anything… *(Beat… slower)*… change it to anything but "now"! It's not me Jo... it's her. I need to go round and see my mum. I don't want her hearing from anyone else...

Jo: Do you want to eat first?

Zinc: Not really. *(Emotionally welling up.)* I'm so sorry love.

(Zinc sees the holiday brochure.)

Zinc: What's this?

Jo: I was going to say then... when you said you'd had an accident I thought... well I thought it would be a nice surprise when you got back... but... well maybe we'd better put it on hold now eh?

Media 5: *Backdrop of a bus shelter.*

Tabs and Emma are sitting waiting for their bus to school. Tabs seems distant and he randomly scrawls onto the glass of the bus stop.

Emma is struggling to hold a conversation with him.

Emma: What's the point of having a bus timetable if they never turn up when they're meant to?

Tabs: Mmm.

Emma: We're gonna be late again. I wanted to stop in the shop before first lesson too...

No response from Tabs

We've got that science mock today as well, we are so going to get done if we're late for that!

Silence. Emma tries to grab his attention.

I know what I forgot to say to you. I went to the doctors the other day, I missed my period ya see. I'm 6 weeks pregnant ya know, with quintuplets, but don't worry they're not yours, I slept with your best mate!

Tabs: Oh right.

Emma: Tabs!

Tabs: What?

Emma: You're not listening to a word I've said! What is up with you this morning?

Tabs: Nothing.

Emma: Yeah right and I'm Leona Lewis!

Tabs: I'm fine.

Emma: I know you too well Tabs! Has it got something to do with that letter?

Tabs: What letter?

Emma: Duh, the one in your pocket, numpty! You keep fiddling with it... come on, spill.

Tabs:　　　It's nothing.

Emma:　　　You won't mind me looking then?

Emma leans over and snatches the letter out of Tabs's pocket.

Tabs:　　　Emma, don't! Give it back yeh.

Emma:　　　You've not even opened it! Who's it from?

Tabs:　　　I don't know?

Emma:　　　Don't give me that! Is this from another girl?

Tabs:　　　What? No!

Emma:　　　Oh my God it is, isn't it?

Emma starts to rip it open to read it.

Tabs:　　　Just give it back!

Emma begins reading the letter aloud.

Emma:　　　"Hiya Dan, long time no see, far too long in fact!" *(Emma glances down at the bottom of the letter to see who it's from)* Who the hell is Kat?

Tabs:　　　My sister.

Emma:　　　What? You never told me you had a sister?

Tabs:　　　You never asked.

Emma:　　　I just assumed… how old is she?

Tabs:　　　She'd be… er… 'bout 19 now.

Emma:　　　Does she drive?

Tabs:　　　What?

Emma:　　　If she does… wouldn't have to wait for buses! *(Laughs)*

Tabs:　　　*(Laughing)* No, don't think so.

Emma:　　　You want me to carry on?

Tabs:　　　Might as well now.

Emma: "I meant to write to you for ages but I've been really busy lately... actually, that's a lie. I mean I have been busy but that's not the reason I've not written. You're a hard man to track down these days. I did contact the Harpers but they said things hadn't worked out and you'd moved on... I hope you're more settled now. " *(To Tabs)* So what happened with you two?

Tabs: Dunno… just kinda lost touch. I ain't seen her in years.

Emma: "I often think about you ya know... all the time... so does Dad... he's changed ya know... "

Tabs gets up and laughs to himself in disbelief, but his laughter quickly turns to anger and he kicks the bus stop in frustration before slumping back down beside.

Emma: What's up with you?

Tabs: Just rip it up eh!

Emma: No.

"Look, I really want us to meet up. I'd really like to sort things between us… all of us...."

Tabs: *(Snatching the letter from Emma and tearing it up.)* I said rip it up!

Emma: What's your problem?

Tabs: Leave it Em!

Emma: Aren't you glad she wants to get back in touch?

Tabs: Em, I'd love to see her again, but I know what she's like, she'll start banging on about my dad again and I ain't interested.

Emma: Don't say that... he's your dad!

Tabs: You don't understand...

Emma: He can't be that bad!?

Tabs: Just change the subject.

Dad:	What's he done then... you still got a cob on 'cause he grounded you once or something?
Tabs:	*(Tabs clearly takes offence)* What! You haven't got a clue Em!
Emma:	Tabs! I'm sorry alright.
Tabs:	Do you really think I'd get this worked up over something that petty!
Emma:	Well I'm sure you can work it all out.
Tabs:	You're forgetting. He abused me Em.
	(Pause)
Emma:	Sorry. *(Pause)* Look, shall we just walk into school... doesn't look like this bus is coming.
Tabs:	You go on... tell them I'm ill or something?
Emma:	Not again Tabs... you'll get proper done... Just come in for a bit yeah?
Tabs:	Nah you're alright.
Emma:	Do you want me to stay with ya?
Tabs:	I'm better on my own for a bit... besides, I don't think bunking really suits you Babe... see you later though yeah? *(He walks off)*
Emma:	*(Calling after him)* Tabs!

Media 6: *Backdrop of Zinc's Lounge.*

Zinc: *(On the phone, with some concern.)* Thanks for letting me know. I am... I'm really sorry.
Yeh... yeh I know.
Bye. *(He puts the phone down and sits down slowly head in hand.)*

(Beat)

Jo: *(Rushing in)* You seen my scissors? I'm trying to wrap Sandy's present and they're not in the drawer... have you had them? Why can't you ever put things back where they belong?

(Pause)

Zed? I'm... *(turning and seeing him for the first time)...* what's up?

Zinc: They switched the life support off at five this morning.

Jo: What? *(Realising)*

Zinc: Poor girl...

(Silence)

Jo: Zed... I'm sorry... I didn't realise... I was just...

Zinc: The scissors... yeh... *(Gets up goes to the place where he thought they might be.)* I... Oh I don't know where I left them, I thought they were... What's the fuck's gonna happen now Jo?

Jo: You've got to be brave.

Zinc: I've "been brave" for the last three bloody weeks! Death by careless driving... I can' t see how I can keep my job... I'm sorry to go on...
I know it's wrong... I know I should think about her... but I can' t help it...

Jo: We've got to concentrate on us... got to find our way through love... they'll have to do the same and their friends will help them. It's my job to look after you and that's what I intend to do.

Silence. Zinc looks up and smiles at Jo. He struggles to pluck up the courage to say is next words.

Zinc:	I can't accept it was my fault though... and I don't think I ever will.
Jo:	Perhaps it'll make them do something... someone's got to do something before it's...
Zinc:	Too late? *(Smiles/laughs... half heartedly)* Is that what you were going to say?
Jo:	Yeh.
Zinc:	I shouldn't laugh. It's wrong but... I don't know what to do... what to say... where to put myself at the moment... I'm like all over the place. I must be terrible to live with. I don't mean to be... this whole thing's changed me.
Jo:	Right. Zed, you've got to do something. Send her family some flowers… or write them a letter… they need to know you're sorry.
Zinc:	That might make it worse for them.
Jo:	You should do something love. *(Pause)* Well?
Zinc:	*(Deep in thought... finally)* Probably.
Jo:	So? What's it to be?
Zinc:	Flowers?
Jo:	OK...
Zinc:	I don't want to deliver them... not me...
Jo:	Internet. Easy.
Zinc:	That'll be OK? *(Jo nods)* Jo, I want to get her song... like download it... do you mind...?
Jo:	Why would I?
Zinc:	You don't think it's wrong do you? It's just something I can do to... you know... support her somehow... without anyone knowing... and this is weird but it'll make me feel like... make me feel close to her somehow. That's not wrong is it?

Media 7: *The video images display the backdrop of a street scene at night.*

The stage is empty apart from a video backdrop projected onto the rear of the acting space. The images depict a quiet street with a bus stop set centrally. Tabs Enters with Emma. She is blindfolded as he guides her towards the bus stop.

Emma: Will you please tell me where we're going?

Tabs: You'll see in a minute.

Emma: Give me a clue then!

Tabs: Um, it's something you can look at...

Emma: How is that a clue?

Tabs: It's a kind of tribute if ya like.

Emma: To who?

Tabs: Posh Spice... who d'ya think!

Media 8: *The video images move to reveal a bus stop with a large graffiti tag sprayed onto it, this then briefly mixed with cctv style images coming from the approaching bus and returns to the bus stop scene.*

Tabs: OK, ready?

Emma: That's it, I'm opening my eyes, but if this isn't worth being...

Emma is stopped in her tracks by what she sees, an elaborate version of Emma's tag on the bus stop.

Tabs: So? What d'ya think?

Emma: My tag! It's amazing!

Tabs: I thought you'd like it.

Emma: I love it.

Tabs: Now all you need to do is to fill it in *(pointing)* there. *(He hands her a can of spray paint. Emma looks round nervously)* Don't worry no one's about... go for it.

Media 9: *The multimedia here becomes interactive. As the actor 'mimes' spraying Emma's name onto the video screen, the graffiti will appear as if really being sprayed real time. The images then briefly flash back to the CCTV images on the bus, and back to the bus stop.*

Emma begins spraying her name beside the tag just as Zinc approaches on his bus. We see CCTV style images projected of the spraying which Zinc is viewing and recording!

Tabs: Oh shit, Em. Hide the can!

Emma: What?

Tabs: The Bus is coming. Just chuck it and let's go.

Emma chucks the can as the bus pulls up. The pair board the bus.

Media 10: *The backdrop of a bus interior at night.*

Emma: Do you think the driver saw me spraying?

Tabs: Nah.

Emma: I reckon he did Tabs. What if he reports it or something?

Tabs: He didn't see Babe.

Emma: Yeah, but what if he did? I wish it had been that matey you knew... your old football coach...

Tabs: If he'd seen you he would have said something wouldn't he.

Emma: Yeah s'pose. That was well close though!

Tabs: Just a bit! A mate of mine got three hundred pound fine for tagging.

Emma: Ouch!

Tabs: Yeah, they're getting well hot on it... operation bus tag they call it!

Emma: You never been caught then?

Tabs: No way, I'm too good Babe.

Emma: *(Laughing)* In your dreams mate.

Tabs: Anyway, let's just hope he don't grass you up... most of them are alright you know.

Emma: Yeh, like that one the other night, tryin' to charge me two quid 'cos I didn't have my Oyster... yeah right, jog on.

Tabs: I reckon he kept the cash and spend it down the pub after his shift. Yeh, I can't see him *(pointing to the driver)* doing anything!

Emma: He'd better not or we'll be right in the shit!

Tabs: Yeh! You would! *(Laughs)*

Emma: Oi you! *(Emma hits him playfully!)*

Media 11: *The multimedia backdrop suddenly morphs into a courtroom scene accompanied by appropriate sound effects and the scene flashes forward to Emma being fined.*

Voiceover 1:   Emma Louise Johnson... in light of the evidence put before this court there is no doubt that on the evening of 18th November you damaged private property by way of graffiti and therefore I have no option other than to convict you of criminal damage. I am imposing a community order and you are ordered to pay costs of £250.

Tabs: But that's not fair, it wasn't her! That driver's a grass.

Voiceover 2:   All Rise.

The sound of a gavel being slammed down echoes into the next scene.

Media 12: *Backdrop of Zinc's lounge.*

Zinc: *(Dressed formally)* Hi love... home. *(Silence)* Jo?

Jo: *(Entering. Dressed for summer.)* Sorry... was in the garden. How did it go?

Zinc: Yeh... helped a lot more than I imagined.

Jo: Thought it would...

Zinc: Go on.

Jo: What?

Zinc: Say "I told you so". *(They laugh)* No, it was good... good for me. Tabs was really, really nice... in the end. He was in tears, poor kid and I had to work hard to keep my feelings under wraps.
It was really emotional. It's hit us both hard.

Jo: I think you're very brave... I know you didn't want to go.

Zinc: He was too. He apologised. He's never grasped what it's been like for me... I mean... he had no idea I'm out of a job. He offered to say something to my boss. He was really shocked I might get prison... and... well... I told him about you and how it's affected us... *(Pause)*... you know.

Jo: What did you say?

Zinc: Quite a lot... I said how... well how it's put a strain on us... both of us... I mean...

Jo: What did he say?

Zinc: He was sorry.

Jo: Did you talk about Kat... sorry, obviously you did... what did he say?

Zinc: It was his fault and he didn't want me to blame myself. He told me how people have been giving him shit saying how he's killed his own sister... I mean really having a go at him... his dad as well. He thinks it's all his fault. I told him that that wasn't the case... and not in the eyes of the law. I should have ignored him...

simple as... just not got involved...
He said he remembered me from football... he said he'd always got on with me... but when he heard the thing about Simon it all got twisted in his brain... cos he thought like I'd been... he wanted me to pay for it... he said he thought I... oh it's stupid...

Jo: He does know you weren't involved in any of it doesn't he?

Zinc: He does now yes... he said how some driver had grassed his girlfriend up for tagging a bus stop and he wanted to get back at him somehow through me... so I said about that kid who graffiti'd our house... and how it took a whole day to get it removed. He was really shocked... and sorry.

Jo: So what happens to him now?

Zinc: The Youth Offending team sort him. They have a program... you know what? I might even do some voluntary work for them... you know... see where it goes from there.

Jo: What?

Zinc: You know how cynical I was about this "restorative justice" thing, but... it was powerful stuff. It sounds soppy but I went to shake his hand after and he looked me straight in the eye and said "Mate, I'm sorry". No one told him to say that Jo. It was real... genuine... and I said sorry to him too... I mean it must be awful for him... both of us had tears in our eyes.

Media 13: *Backdrop of the local park.*

Emma:	Sorry I took so long.
Tabs:	I'm surprised your dad let you out!
Emma:	He didn't. *(Tabs laughs)* He'll calm down… he always does.
Tabs:	I wish I'd never done that stupid tag now.
Emma:	I'm glad! No one's ever done anything like that for me before.
Tabs:	Look where it's got us though.
Emma:	Things'll get better, I promise.
Tabs:	They can't get much worse! Hey, I was thinking what you said the other day… about meeting up with Kat... she's got a record deal and everything.
Emma:	Truth?
Tabs:	Yeah… got some press thing to launch her first single. She sent me another letter, with the CD in.
Emma:	What's it like?
Tabs:	Sick! Weird to think it's my sister's voice, I forgot what she sounded like... but get this!
Emma:	What?
Tabs:	The song's about me.
Emma:	How do you mean?
Tabs:	She says it's about her being frustrated 'cos she wants to see me and I keep on pushing her away. 's called Driven to Distraction…
Emma:	Wicked! That she's written a song about you I mean.
Tabs:	Yeh, guess so.
Emma:	You gonna speak to her then?
Tabs:	I texted her yesterday. I've told her I do wanna meet.

Emma:	Finally seeing sense eh? Men! ... Oh my God! I forgot to say... you know that TV show...
Tabs:	You might have to narrow it down a bit for me Babe!
Emma:	You know that music quiz thing, Never Mind the Buzzcocks?
Tabs:	Yeah.
Emma:	You'll never guess who was on there?
Tabs:	Who?
Emma:	That Bus Driver!
Tabs:	The one that grassed you up?
Emma:	No, the coach... your footie team... yeah well anyway, he was on it, ya know, in that line up they do where you have to guess who was the member in the band.
Tabs:	Seriously?
Emma:	Yeah, his names Zinc or something, he used to be in a band back in the 80's, Hungry... something or other... with Simon Kent! He looked a right numpty back then!
Tabs:	Weren't they the paedophiles or something? Aww mate that's sick, letting some kiddy fiddler coach a kids footy team.
Emma:	No Tabs, he was just the guitarist... Zinc Alloyd or something... that's why they call him Zed. Simon Kent was the paedo. Zed was nothing to do with all that or they wouldn't have had him on telly would they?
Tabs:	I don't know Em, seems a bit odd doesn't it? Why would someone like that wanna coach a kids footy team?
Emma:	He probably just wanted to do something useful when the band was finished.
Tabs:	You are so gullible.
Emma:	Don't call me that.

Tabs:	Well you are.
Emma:	Tabs!
Tabs:	The perv probably got some kind of thrill out of it.
Emma:	Now you're just being stupid! He was just the guitarist Tabs. Just cos the lead singer was a perv doesn't mean that the rest of the band were too. It's stupid rumours like that that get out of hand.
Tabs:	Yeah, well you think what you like Babe.
Emma:	I will.
Tabs:	Good.
Emma:	Good.

Media 14: *Backdrop of Zinc's Lounge.*

Zinc:	That was Mike...
Jo:	What was?
Zinc:	The phone.
Jo:	Didn't hear it? Mike from the reality show thing?
Zinc:	Yeh... they want an answer by the end of the day.
Jo:	And?
Zinc:	Still not sure.
Jo:	You know what I think.
Zinc:	It's not my kind of thing love...
Jo:	Then why haven't you already turned them down?
Zinc:	Because I know you want me to do it.
Jo:	You'd like your name out there again wouldn't you?
Zinc:	Not right now.
Jo:	It's a lot of money... could end up being a massive amount... and lead to other stuff... and at the moment everyone's on your side...
Zinc:	The local press is not "everyone"!
Jo:	You're this "have a go hero". It could kick start your music again... you'd love that if it did, wouldn't you?!
Zinc:	"If"... yeh...
Jo:	You can put your side forward.
Zinc:	My side isn't very interesting. I knew nothing! Anyway these things are edited to max the viewing figures... they just want good telly!
Jo:	You are good telly! Your views on Simon would be for sure!
Zinc:	I'll say the wrong thing and end up in more trouble!

Jo:	Look, my parents have bailed us out for the last few months... willingly... but that can't go on forever. I'm doing my management course and that will lead to something sometime... but we need money now. You have your past... we can trade with that... it's our only hope.
Zinc:	I was just a guitarist in a group!
Jo:	In Hungry Wolf for God's sake! Anyway, when Simon left you...
Zinc:	But it only got to number 18...
Jo:	It was the first Hungry Wolf song I'd ever heard, so for me you were the lead singer... I didn't even know about Simon...
Zinc:	Be careful Jo... you're getting all dewey eyed!
Jo:	I don't think there's any danger of that right now!
	(Silence)
Zinc:	Jo?
Jo:	I didn't mean it like that.
	(Pause)
Zinc:	There's something else Mike said that worries me.
Jo:	What?
Zinc:	Simon's likely to be released the week the show goes out.
Jo:	I thought he was in for life!
Zinc:	That's what Mike said.
Jo:	No wonder they want you... it could be huge Zed...
Zinc:	Yeh, but people won't suddenly want to hear our music... if anything it'll turn them off.
Jo:	You haven't done anything wrong!

Zinc:	Yeh, but Simon did! Guilt by association Jo! I mean why hasn't there ever been any interest in a tribute band?
Jo:	People will be intrigued though... they'll want to know what you think!
Zinc:	They just want me to say how terrible he is... and it's not as simple as that... even that sounds all wrong, like I'm supporting what he did... I didn't know what he was up to... how many more times! Look, the bottom line is I don't want it all dragged up again, it seems to be incriminating to have been in his band!

(Pause)

	Jo... that meeting with Tabs... it kind of healed lots of stuff for me... and... well... I don't want... I just can't have his family saying I'm profiting out of her death, can't you see that?
Jo:	It's Hungry Wolf that made you a celebrity!
Zinc:	An ex-celebrity until all the fuss about the crash.
Jo:	The "celebrity" comes from Hungry Wolf and not from the crash... the crash just...
Zinc:	What?
Jo:	Was an angle for the media... Kat's people used it didn't they... she would never have had a number one without it! Well she wouldn't! They used it, so why can't you?
Zinc:	It's not the same!
Jo:	It wasn't your fault!
Zinc:	So why have I lost my job then?
Jo:	You just lie down and accept everything don't you?
Zinc:	No!
Jo:	You bloody do!

Zinc:	Jo, please, I'm trying to move on... I don't want to spend the rest of my life looking back!
Jo:	You're always bloody talking about it... waking up in bed telling me you've had a nightmare... now you're trying to deny it's there... come on Zed... face up!
	(*Silence*)
	You won't get this kind of offer twice!
Zinc:	I don't want to do it love.
Jo:	So... what do we do?
Zinc:	I'll phone and tell them I don't want to do it... I don't... I'm sorry!
Jo:	Wait. We can't go on like this... nor can my parents.
Zinc:	What are you saying?
Jo:	This is our best... our only chance!
	(*Pause*)
	The truth is Zed... you don't have the guts!
Zinc:	And are you really ready for all the crap that'll be thrown up?
Jo:	I mean it Zed... it's our only chance.

Tabs is sitting in front a computer screen, surfing the internet to find stories about Hungry Wolf, Simon Kent and Zinc.

Music 4 / Media 15: *The searches Tabs makes are displayed via multimedia which includes a series of mock up newspaper clipping of the Paedophile story and accompanied by eighties style music. Tabs frantically searches, finding more and more information about Zinc and the band. As his search comes to an end the final article is about Hungry Wolf losing everything. An email icon then pops up on Tabs's screen. He open's the email... it's from Kat.*

Tabs: *(Reading the email aloud.)* Hey little bro, I'm glad you got bk to me. I would have loved 2 have met up 2morrow but I've got dat press launch babe, remember? How bout the day afta, we'll meet in town 4 a coffee or somethin' yeah? I can't wait, All my love, Kat. xx

Tabs closes the lid of his laptop and smiles. He seems really happy.

Media 16: A backdrop of a street scene, daytime.

Emma and Tabs enter. Tabs is playing with a water pistol.

Emma:	What did you get that for?
Tabs:	Aww, not scared of a little water are you? *(He squirts her – and in the process some of the audience!)*
Emma:	Oh, not in my hair you nonce!
Tabs:	Who you calling a nonce, eh? *(Tabs squirts Emma and chases her. They wrestle one another to the ground until Emma manages to prise the water pistol from Tabs and she turns it on him.)*
Emma:	Ah ha, not so big now are ya!
Tabs:	Hey, now don't do anything stupid OK, just put the water pistol down and let's talk about it OK.
Emma:	Alright, I'm putting it down very slowly OK.
Tabs:	Good girl.
Emma:	I lied. *(Emma soaks Tabs as he prises it back out of her hands.)*
Tabs:	That was out of order!
Emma:	Where did you get it anyway?
Tabs:	In the shop when I got my drink… a pound… bargain!
Emma:	You big kid.
Tabs:	You love it!

Media 17: Media here show's the view from the bus from the drivers perspective as it approaches a stop and then changes to a backdrop of a bus stop and then changes once more to show the interior of the bus as Tabs and Emma sit down.

(The sound of a bus engine running. Zinc is standing on another part of the stage.)

Zinc:	Just my luck to be on duty that day. Number 5. Romford to Barking. As I approached the stop on the High Road I saw two kids and an elderly gent. The kids were messing around so I knew it might be "interesting" so to speak... they had a water pistol... so, to avoid anything nasty I decided to just keep an eye out. Apart from anything else, I had a couple of kids from the local... special school on board... I'm always wary of them being picked on... it happens... then, as they climbed on the bus *(They approach Zinc)* I realised the lad was none other than Tabs, the little footballer I'd known from my Parkside Dodgers days. I expected him to be pleased to bump into me again I guess... but... instead he made a very odd remark:
Tabs:	Got a pen mate?
Zinc:	Why?
Tabs:	I ain't ever had a pop star's autograph before. *(Tabs and Emma laugh).*
Zinc:	Saw the Buzzcocks then?
Tabs:	Course I did... and that's not all I've seen Zinc! Kept that one quiet, eh?
Zinc:	Well you were young... you wouldn't have heard of them would you?
Tabs:	Have now though.
Zinc:	Yeh... um, Oysters? *(Emma shows her Oyster card and makes her way to the back of the lower deck. Zinc turns to Tabs.)* Where's yours?
Tabs:	I've got it!
Zinc:	He fumbled about for a bit then produced it as though he was in some magic show! This wasn't the Tab's I'd encountered more recently, this time he had an air of trouble about him... he put me on edge... they both did.
Tabs:	Teh dah! *(Tabs does a big flourish as he produces the card!)*

Emma:	Come on Tabs! *(He heads off towards the seat.)*
Zinc:	They both went and sat down on the lower deck… just where I didn't want them to sit…just a few rows behind the you know… the kids.
Tabs:	Put your foot down Zincy Boy!
Emma:	*(Laughing and hitting him playfully.)* Shut up!
Zinc:	At first I thought he was just talking a bit loud… ya know, just to be annoying… then I realised it was a bit more than that:
Tabs:	*(Talking to Emma but referring to Zinc and speaking louder than necessary so Zinc can hear.)* Did you hear about that Simon Kent. He got done for the child porn stuff, apparently his guitarist mate is a bus driver now…
Zinc:	I knew I had to ignore it… but it was impossible!
Tabs:	*(Still talking loudly.)* Fancy being mates with someone who does that and not saying anything. It's wrong!

(Emma is playfully hitting Tabs and telling him to shut up. Tabs squirts his gun up in the air.)

Media 18: CCTV Images show a water pistol being squirted at the screen, then flashes back to the backdrop of the bus interior, the images in this section maybe change from the interior view, to the CCTV view to an exterior view of the bus in motion.

Zinc:	I looked up at the screen and it was then I saw the young lad flashing the water pistol around and squirting the CCTV camera.
Emma:	Stop it Tabs…
Tabs:	Not doing any harm!
Emma:	You'll get us chucked off!
Tabs:	He wouldn't dare.
Emma:	He might.
Tabs:	You heard what they said in court that day… these drivers can't leave their cabs. They're not allowed to.

Zinc:	I saw one passenger move away. It was about this time that we moved onto a small section of the road that's on a dual carriageway. The traffic was flowing easily… we were doing about forty miles an hour. There was a silver merc in front of me… I remember that… Simon Kent had an early version of it all those years ago…
Tabs:	*(Now speaking quite loud.)* Do you reckon that guitarist ever… ya know… had a go himself?
Emma:	Tabs, it's not funny!
Tabs:	Shut up! *(He squirts her in the face playfull.)* I heard he works with a kids football team in Parkside.
Emma:	*(Squeals and grabs the pistol.)* Give it here! *(She squirts him and Tabs runs towards middle of the bus.)*
Zinc:	Get back in your seat, it's not a playground!
Tabs:	Bet you wish it was. *(Tabs laughs)*
Zinc:	I said, turn it in, there's other passengers on the bus.
Tabs:	Or what?
Zinc:	A real atmosphere was brewing… it was horrible. One of the girls from the school seemed to be… I dunno… tearful…
Tabs:	Come on Zed… or is it Zinc… Zinc Alloyd… I know who you are. So what are you going to do about it you paedo?
Zinc:	Oy! Sit down!

Media 19: CCTV Images flash quickly and mix with other shot of the interior and exterior, these images then become distorted as the bus crashes.

(Zinc looks in his mirror/screen and sees Tabs approaching his Cab. Dramatic music builds up to a climax and then merges with the sounds of a crash. The three characters on stage physically illustrate the whiplash effect caused by the impact of the crash and the car smashing into the scaffolding. Multimedia images become distorted. Tabs is thrown to the floor and Emma slumps on a seat.)

A suggestion for this scene is that the actors voices are recorded repeating various lines from the play and then these can be played back over the crash sequence with echo effects added. These lines can also build up to a climax up to the point of impact. They freeze.

Media 20: The media here show's a street with traffic moving slowly, sirens can be heard in the distance. The lines below can either be pre-recorded and played out with added echo effects, or simply spoken by the actors. The stillness in this section should contrast greatly to the manic build up to the crash.

Police woman: Tabs, we've got some dreadful news. The girl in the accident... we're really sorry to have to say this. She was your sister...

Jo: Every day you come home with horror stories... being abused... spat at... eggs... stones hurled at the bus... I mean golf clubs one time you said!

Zinc: They switched the life support off.

The lights fade to black.

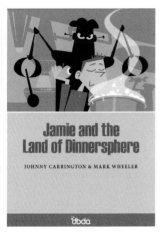

ISBN 978 1 902843 25 4

Cast: 2m and 2f with doubling or 3m, 1f and 5 or 6m/f. Suitable for use as a TIE production in the new vocational courses for ages 13+ (or as a performance piece in Primary schools)
Duration: 35 minutes (55 minutes with the workshop)

Jamie and the Land of Dinnersphere (a Healthy school dinners play)
by Johnny Carrington & Mark Wheeller

Jamie Jamjar loves healthy food. He has seen how a poor diet can mess you up… just by looking at his sister… Lazy Lillian! Jamie is shocked when his school tries out the new Robot Dudes (fast food servants) who replace the friendly dinner ladies. Jamie then discovers his own father invented them!

Can it get any worse? Yes it can!

Jamie is transported to Dinnersphere (in another of his father's inventions, a Story Rocket) where Jamie discovers the nefarious Dinnerwitch, busy planning world domination through putrid school dinners! Together with three friends, Bo, Agor and another - a member of the Primary School audience - they confront and defeat the Dinnerwitch!

Jamie provides an opportunity for secondary school students to present an interactive Theatre In Education play with all the joys of the audience being a key part of the final performance. It is expected to become a staple part of the new vocational courses where there are, at the moment, few plays which will fit the specification so well!

The text includes an innovative interactive workshop written by Adrian New (Stopwatch Theatre) which can be led by the secondary students.

Other plays published by **dbda**

ISBN 978 1 902843 20 9

Cast: 11+ (3m, 3f & 5 m or f)
*Suitable for GCSE with doubling
(2m, 2f & 1 m or f)*
Duration: *50 minutes approx.*
Suitable for: *ages 13+ or
adults!*

*Commissioned and
premiered by The
Birmingham Rep Theatre*

KILL JILL by Mark Wheeller

Big Brother meets Kill Bill meets Jack
(of Beanstalk fame) meets Tony Martin...
Mix these together to create *Kill Jill!* This
brand new play by Mark Wheeller explores
the topical issues of homeowners defending
themselves, and asks "How far can Reality TV
be allowed to go?"

Jill is the latest victim of Reality Lottery,
a futuristic form of National Service to
entertainment. She accompanies Jack as he
(again) robs George, who lies in wait armed
with a shotgun. The Reality Lottery camera
operators are filming everything... but
should they intervene? The ending is suitably
Tarantinoesque!

Kill Jill! raises issues of rights and
responsibilities. It is a play full of interesting
techniques that will delight Drama teachers
and students, and will thrill those exploring
Citizenship issues through imaginative and
entertaining Theatre productions.

'Kill Jill is a very fizzy ride! What a great
script! The playfulness with style and wide
range of reference points with an 'anytime,
anyplace, anywhere' theatrical freedom...
the banter goes to some strange places
too - perhaps a Python influence? The build
up of tension in the visit to George's castle
puts the end of the play in firm thriller
territory! Wonderful stuff!!!!!'

*Paul Mills, Head of Drama,
Westgate School, Winchester*

ISBN 978 1 902843 26 1

Cast: 6 (3m, 3f with doubling).
Can be performed with a cast
of up to around 30. (10m, 8f &
12 m or f)
Duration: 55 minutes
Suitable for: ages 13+
or adults!

*Developed from Mark
Wheeller's stage play Race
To Be Seen, written with the
Epping Youth Theatre.*

Available on DVD, the
award winning Oaklands
Youth Theatre production.
*For more information
contact dbda.*

Graham – World's Fastest Blind Runner! by Mark Wheeller

Written in the same documentary style as Too
Much Punch For Judy, Mark's first version of
this play about Graham Salmon MBE, was
awarded Critics Choice at the Edinburgh
Festival Fringe (1984).

It has recently been re-written, and on it's first
two outings won through to the Final of both
the National Drama Festivals Association in
2007 and the All England Theatre Festival in
2008, winning different awards at each Festival.

Listed in the Guiness Book of Records as The
Worlds Fastest Blind Runner in 1976 (100m in
11.4 secs) Graham went on to play Golf for
the international visually impaired team for
whom he hit a famous "hole in one" in The
British Open!

"I didn't ever need convincing that 'Graham' was
an ideal piece to challenge my group and that
it ticked all the boxes for A-level work, but if I
ever needed justification, then the results have
certainly given it. In the breakdown of the Unit 2
marks i.e. the performance of 'Graham', all seven
candidates were awarded 100%. It's worth noting
that the external moderator was accompanied
that evening by her senior examiner! Thanks again
for the material and thanks to Graham, such an
inspirational person!"

Mike Fleetwood, Parkside Arts College.

Selected as an exemplar Unit 2 study text in the
Longman/Pearson 2009 Edexcel GCSE Drama
Teacher and Student book.

ISBN 1 902843 19 3

Cast: *34m, 3f & 2m/f or 2m & 2f for GCSE*
Duration: *35 minutes approx.*
KS 3 & 4

Chicken! by Mark Wheeller

A 'new and improved' version of WHY DID THE CHICKEN CROSS THE ROAD? The play tells the story of two cousins, Tammy and Chris. We are led to believe that something bad will happen to Chris who refuses to wear his cycle helmet. It is, however, Tammy who gets killed on the one morning that the cousins walk to school. Chris remains unwilling to tell anyone of his part in the accident and he has to live with this dreadful secret. One of the main changes is the introduction of Chris filming Tammy's fatal dare on his mobile phone camera.

'We have just been fortunate enough to witness the most superb exhibition of interactive safety education. The performance was quite stunning!'

Jim Lambert, Head Teacher Sinclair Middle School, Southampton

---

ISBN 978 1 902843 08 7

Cast: *3f & 2m with doubling, or 6f, 3m & 16*
Duration: *70 minutes approx.*
KS 3 to adult

Hard to Swallow by Mark Wheeller

This play is an adaptation of Maureen Dunbar's award winning book (and film) **Catherine** which charts her daughter's uneven battle with anorexia and the family's difficulties in coping with the illness.

The play has gone on to be performed all over the world to much acclaim, achieving considerable success in One Act Play Festivals. Its simple narrative style means that it is equally suitable for adult and older youth groups to perform.

'This play reaches moments of almost unbearable intensity... naturalistic scenes flow seamlessly into sequences of highly stylised theatre... such potent theatre!'
Vera Lustiq, The Independent

'Uncompromising and sensitive... should be compulsory viewing to anyone connected with the education of teenagers.'

Mick Martin, Times Educational Supplement

The Gate Escape by Mark Wheeller

The story of two truants. Corey is 'addicted' to bunking school. Chalkie views himself as a casual truant "no problem!" While truanting with some friends, the pair are greeted by a surreal 'Big Brother' figure who sets them a task. The loser will be in for some dramatic 'Big Bother'... Who will lose?... What will this 'bother' be?

The play has toured professionally throughout the south of England to great acclaim.

'A lively dramatic style and innovative structure with dynamic and contemporary dialogue. It is written in a way to guarantee that the audience will feel fully involved and enthralled by the main characters.'

Professor Ken Reid, Author of Tackling Truancy in Schools

'Theatrically interesting... excellent basis for active discussion of issues and dramatic style with reluctant GCSE students'

Ali Warren (National Drama)

ISBN 978 1 902843 22 3

Cast: *2f & 2m with doubling, or up to 30*
Duration: *70 minutes*
KS 3 & 4

Heroin Lies by Wayne Denfhy

A sensitive, yet disturbing look at drugs and drug dependency, in particular the pressures and influences at play on an ordinary teenage girl. We observe Vicki's gradual and tragic slide towards addiction and also the various degrees of help and hindrance she receives from family and friends.

This is a new, updated edition of Wayne Denfhy's popular play. It is suitable for performance as well as for reading in the class. Included with the playscript is an excellent scheme for follow-up work by Peter Rowlands.

'...a piece of drama that will stimulate and challenge a young cast... Heroin Lies deals with vital issues that affect today's youngsters in a gentle and humane way and, in so doing, gets its message across without the instant rejection that can meet other approaches.'

Pete Sanpher, Head of Drama, Norfolk

ISBN 1 902843 15 0

Cast: *8f, 7m and 2m/f*
Duration: *70 minutes approx.*
KS 3 & 4

Other plays published by **dbda**

ISBN 978 1 902843 21 6
Cast: 2m & 2f
Suitable for GCSE
Duration: 55 minutes approx.
KS 3 & 4

Bang Out Of Order
by Johnny Carrington & Danny Sturrock

4 friends, 1 secret, 1 chance, 1 life. The play tackles
anti-social behaviour head on. This rollercoaster ride
will educate, amuse and challenge.

Set on an urban estate, newcomer Ollie has a history
of antisocial behaviour and is attempting to reform.
His family are forced to move away in an attempt to
make a fresh start… but once he is accepted into the
local group of youths, things start to go wrong.

The play tackles the sensitive issues using a mixture
of comedy, dance, music and multi-media.

'If you are setting out to convey a message, the
mixture of naturalism which pulls no punches,
stylised movement that moves the action along with
wit and mixed media, adds another dimension that
certainly grabs the attention of the audience.'

Fran Morley, Director, Nuffield Theatre Southampton

ISBN 978 1 902843 16 2
Cast: 2m & 2f with doubling,
or up to 18
Duration: 45-50 minutes
KS 3 to adult

Missing Dan Nolan by Mark Wheeller

This play, based on the true story of Dan Nolan,
a teenage boy who went missing on the night of
January 1st 2002, is written in the same documentary
style as Too Much Punch for Judy. It has won awards
and commendations at every Drama Festival it has
entered. It is now, like so many of Mark's other plays
being toured professionally by the Queens Theatre
Hornchurch, Essex.

'Unusual and deeply affecting. Skillfully written…
achieves astonishing depth and authenticity… '

Charles Evans, Adjudicator, Eastleigh Drama Festival

Exemplar text for Unit 2 in the Hodder Education
Edexcel Drama for GCSE book (2009 specification)
endorsed by Edexcel.

Gagging for it by Danny Sturrock

Summer is here, A-levels are over and a group of 6 friends embark on a holiday to Ibiza! What would their holiday bring? Would Chris finally pluck up the courage to ask out Teresa? Would Jay drink himself into oblivion? Would Bianca spend the entire holiday flirting with the Spanish barmen – more than likely! …or would their experiments with drugs bring their hedonistic worlds crashing down around them!?

Comedy, dance, music and choreography are the keys to this production. The pace is breakneck and hilarious, but once the party's over, it hits you!

'Really funny… laugh out loud funny. Inspired outstanding performances from the six Year 11s who went on to exceed our expectations by a long way in their GCSEs achieving A or A*. It proved to be a firm favourite with our KS3/4 audience.'

Mark Wheeller

ISBN 1 902843 17 7

Cast: 33f, 3m &3m/f or 3m & 3f for GCSE using suggested cuts
Duration: 55 minutes approx.
KS 3 & 4

Legal Weapon II by Mark Wheeller

This is a new "improved" version of the popular Legal Weapon play which is touring schools across the UK.

It is the story of a young man, Andy. His relationship with his girlfriend – and his car – are both flawed, but his speeding causes the loss of a life and the loss of his freedom.

In Legal Weapon II, the story takes an additional twist when Andy realises that the person he's killed is somebody very dear to Jazz, his girlfriend.

Legal Weapon II promises to be faster, funnier and far more powerful!

'A gripping storyline. Even the most challenging of our students were held by the drama. This learning experience should be given to each Year 11 as they come through the school.'

Myrtle Springs Secondary School

ISBN 978 1 902843 18 6

Cast: 32f & 2m with doubling
Duration: 60 minutes approx.
KS 3 & 4 and A Level

Other plays published by **dbda**

Script & Lyrics by Mark Wheeller
Music by James Holmes

Wacky Soap

The Music Score

Includes a Mini-Musical for Junior Schools

ISBN 1 902843 06 1

The full version of the Musical play which includes scheme of work for KS3/4.

Wacky Soap by Mark Wheeller

Wacky Soap is a Pythonesque allegorical tale about 'substance' abuse (drugs, alcohol, glue, tobacco, etc). While washing with Wacky Soap leads to instant happiness and an inclination towards outrageous behaviour, prolonged use washes away limbs and ultimately leads to dematerialisation. This has become a tried and tested (and increasingly popular School/ Drama Club/ Youth Theatre production and is an ideal vehicle for a cast of any age.

'Wacky Soap is a brilliant show for any age group. It has the "Wow factor" not the "Yawn factor" so often associated with educational material. The script is fast and comical. The songs are wonderful catchy. The Audience at the end were calling for more'.

*Sally Dwyer, Hants Drama Teacher
Eastleigh Borough Youth Theatre Director*

The story of Wacky Soap first appeared as a full **Musical play.** A mini version of the play is included with the **Music Score**. The **Storybook**, as well as being a wonderful book to read on its own, is often used for inspiration with props and costumes for the play. **A Past-performance CD** gives you the opportunity to hear the songs of the play, while a fully orchestrated **Backing track CD** is invaluable for those who want to produce the play but do not have music facilities.

The Story of
WACKY SOAP
A Cautionary Tale

Mark & Rachael Wheeller
Illustrations by Geoffrey Griggs

ISBN 1 902843 07 X

A fully illustrated book with the story of Wacky Soap in narrative form.

Wacky Soap
A Cautionary Tale

SCRIPT & LYRICS BY MARK WHEELLER
MUSIC BY JAMES HOLMES

dbda

ISBN 1 902843 02 9

*A companion book with the Music Score and a **Mini-Musical** version of the play.*

Past Performance and Backing track CDs